Brownies Cookbook

Delicious and Easy to Make Recipes, Easy to Find Ingredients

Delores Levi

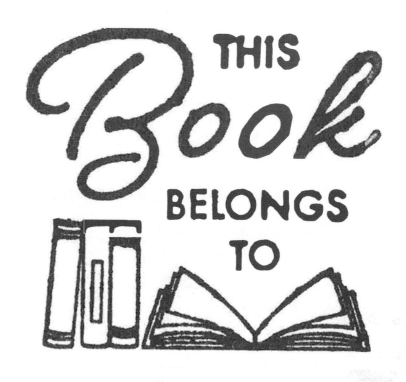

THIS **Book** BELONGS TO

....

Thank you for Purchasing my book and taking the time to read it from front to back. I am always grateful when a reader chooses my work and I hope you enjoyed it!

With the vast selection available online, I am touched that you chose to be purchasing my work and take valuable time out of your life to read it. My hope is that you feel you made the right decision.

I very much would like to know what you thought of the book. Please take the time to write an honest and informative review on Amazon.com. Your experience and opinions will be of great benefit to me and those readers looking to make an informed choice.

With much thanks.

Table of Contents

Summary

Celebrating the Richness and Diversity of Brownies: Brownies, those delectable treats that have captured the hearts and taste buds of people all around the world. From their humble beginnings as a simple chocolate dessert, brownies have evolved into a rich and diverse range of flavors, textures, and variations. Today, we celebrate the richness and diversity of brownies, exploring the different types and ingredients that make them so irresistible.

One of the most iconic types of brownies is the classic fudgy brownie. These brownies are dense, moist, and incredibly chocolatey. They have a gooey texture that melts in your mouth, leaving you craving for more. The secret to achieving this fudgy perfection lies in the ratio of butter to flour. By using a higher proportion of butter, the brownies become more moist and rich, resulting in that signature fudgy texture.

On the other end of the spectrum, we have the cakey brownie. These brownies are lighter and fluffier in texture, resembling a traditional chocolate cake. They have a slightly drier consistency compared to their fudgy counterparts, but are equally delicious. The key to achieving a cakey brownie lies in the leavening agents, such as baking powder or baking soda, which help the brownies rise and create that airy texture.

For those who prefer a little crunch in their brownies, there are the chewy brownies. These brownies have a slightly crispy exterior, while still maintaining a soft and chewy center. The addition of nuts, such as walnuts or pecans, adds a delightful crunch and enhances the overall flavor profile. The combination of textures in chewy brownies creates a truly satisfying eating experience.

But the richness and diversity of brownies doesn't stop there. There are countless variations and additions that can take brownies to a whole new level. From swirling in cream cheese for a marbled effect, to adding caramel or peanut butter for an extra layer of indulgence, the possibilities are endless. Brownies can also be infused with different flavors, such as mint, orange, or even coffee, to create unique and exciting taste experiences.

Furthermore, brownies can cater to various dietary preferences and restrictions. For those who follow a gluten-free diet, there are brownie recipes that use alternative flours, such as almond or coconut flour, to create a delicious gluten-free option. Vegans can also enjoy the richness of brownies by substituting traditional ingredients with plant-based alternatives, such as coconut oil or apples

The Universal Appeal and Variations of Brownies: Brownies are a universally loved dessert that has a wide appeal across different cultures and regions. This delectable treat is known for its rich, fudgy texture and irresistible chocolate flavor. Whether enjoyed as a standalone dessert or paired with a scoop of ice cream, brownies are a go-to indulgence for many people.

One of the reasons why brownies have such a universal appeal is their versatility. While the classic brownie recipe calls for a simple combination of butter, sugar, eggs, flour, and cocoa powder, there are countless variations that cater to different tastes and dietary preferences. From adding nuts or chocolate chips to incorporating ingredients like peanut butter, caramel, or even fruits, the possibilities for customization are endless. This allows individuals to tailor their brownies to their liking, making them a dessert that can be enjoyed by everyone.

Furthermore, brownies are a dessert that transcends cultural boundaries. While they are often associated with American cuisine, brownies have found their way into the hearts and stomachs of people all around the world. In fact, variations of brownies can be found in many different countries, each with their own unique twist. For example, in Mexico, there is a type of brownie called chocolate abuelita brownies that incorporates Mexican chocolate and cinnamon for a spicy kick. In Japan, matcha green tea brownies are popular, showcasing the country's love for this traditional ingredient. These international variations highlight the adaptability of brownies and their ability to be enjoyed by people from diverse backgrounds.

Another reason for the universal appeal of brownies is their simplicity. Unlike more complex desserts that require intricate techniques and lengthy preparation times, brownies are relatively easy to make. With just a few basic ingredients and a simple mixing process, anyone can whip up a batch of brownies in no time. This accessibility makes brownies a popular choice for both experienced bakers and beginners alike, ensuring that everyone can enjoy this delicious treat.

In addition to their simplicity, brownies also have a nostalgic quality that resonates with people of all ages. Many people have fond memories of baking brownies with their parents or grandparents, or enjoying them at school bake sales or birthday parties. This sentimental attachment to brownies adds to their universal appeal, as they evoke feelings of comfort and happiness.

In conclusion, the universal appeal of brownies can be attributed to their versatility, cultural adaptability, simplicity, and nostalgic charm. Whether enjoyed in their classic form or with unique variations, brown

Purpose and Structure of Brownies: The purpose of brownies is to provide a delicious and indulgent treat that can be enjoyed by people of all ages. Brownies are a type of baked dessert that are typically made with chocolate, butter, sugar, eggs, and flour. They are known for their rich and fudgy texture, and are often enjoyed with a glass of milk or a scoop of ice cream.

The structure of brownies is what gives them their unique and desirable characteristics. The ingredients are combined and mixed together to create a thick and smooth batter. This batter is then poured into a baking dish and baked in the oven until it is set and slightly firm to the touch. The baking process allows the brownies to develop a crispy top layer, while the inside remains moist and gooey.

The key to achieving the perfect brownie structure lies in the balance of ingredients and the baking time. The amount of chocolate used can greatly affect the texture and flavor of the brownies. Using high-quality chocolate with a high cocoa content will result in a more intense and rich chocolate flavor. The butter adds moisture and richness to the brownies, while the sugar provides sweetness and helps to create a slightly crispy exterior.

Eggs are an essential ingredient in brownies as they help to bind the other ingredients together and add structure to the final product. The flour acts as a stabilizer and helps to give the brownies their structure. It is important not to overmix the batter once the flour is added, as this can result in a tougher and less tender brownie.

The baking time and temperature are crucial in achieving the desired texture of brownies. Overbaking can lead to dry and crumbly brownies, while underbaking can result in a gooey and undercooked center. It is important to keep a close eye on the brownies while they are baking and to test for doneness by inserting a toothpick into the center. If it comes out with a few moist crumbs clinging to it, the brownies are done.

In conclusion, the purpose of brownies is to provide a delicious and indulgent treat that can be enjoyed by people of all ages. The structure of brownies is achieved through the balance of ingredients and the baking process. The combination of chocolate, butter, sugar, eggs, and flour creates a rich and fudgy texture, while the baking time and temperature ensure that the brownies are cooked to perfection. Whether enjoyed on their own or with a scoop of ice cream, brownies

How to Use This Cookbook to Create Opulent Brownie Delights: Welcome to our cookbook! We are excited to share with you our recipes for creating opulent brownie delights. In this guide, we will provide you with step-by-step instructions on how to use this cookbook effectively to make the most decadent and mouthwatering brownies you've ever tasted.

First and foremost, it's important to familiarize yourself with the layout of this cookbook. We have organized the recipes into different sections based on the type of brownie you want to create. Whether you're in the mood for classic fudgy brownies, rich and gooey caramel brownies, or even indulgent cheesecake brownies, we have a recipe for every brownie lover out there.

Once you have chosen the type of brownie you want to make, take a moment to read through the recipe from start to finish. This will give you an overview of the ingredients and equipment you will need, as well as the steps involved in the baking process. It's always a good idea to gather all your ingredients and measure them out before you begin, as this will make the baking process much smoother.

Next, pay close attention to any special instructions or tips provided in the recipe. These can often be found in the recipe introduction or in separate sections throughout the recipe. These tips are designed to help you achieve the best possible results and may include suggestions for ingredient substitutions, variations, or techniques to enhance the flavor and texture of your brownies.

As you start preparing the batter, make sure to follow the instructions carefully. Baking is a science, and even the smallest deviations from the recipe can affect the final outcome. Pay attention to details such as the order in which ingredients are added, the mixing techniques required, and the baking time and temperature specified. These details are crucial for achieving the perfect brownie texture and flavor.

Once your brownies are in the oven, resist the temptation to open the oven door too frequently. Opening the door can cause fluctuations in temperature, which can affect the baking process and result in unevenly cooked brownies. Instead, rely on the suggested baking time and use a toothpick or cake tester to check for doneness. Insert it into the center of the brownies, and if it comes out with a few moist crumbs clinging to it, your brownies are ready to be taken out of the oven.

After removing the brownies from the oven, allow them to cool completely before cutting and serving. This will ensure that they set properly and maintain their shape.

Understanding the Core Ingredients of Brownies: Brownies are a beloved dessert that has been enjoyed by people all over the world for many years. They are known for their rich, chocolatey flavor and dense, fudgy texture. While there are many variations of brownie recipes, there are a few core ingredients that are essential to creating the perfect brownie.

The first and most important ingredient in brownies is chocolate. The type of chocolate used can greatly affect the flavor and texture of the brownies. Most recipes call for unsweetened chocolate or cocoa powder, which provides a deep, intense chocolate flavor. Some recipes also include semisweet or bittersweet chocolate, which adds a touch of sweetness and richness to the brownies. The chocolate is typically melted and combined with other ingredients to create a smooth, velvety batter.

Another key ingredient in brownies is butter. Butter not only adds flavor to the brownies, but it also helps to create a moist and tender texture. Most recipes call for unsalted butter, as it allows for better control of the overall saltiness of the brownies. The butter is typically melted and combined with the chocolate to create a smooth, creamy mixture.

Sugar is another essential ingredient in brownies. It not only adds sweetness, but it also helps to create a chewy texture. Most recipes call for granulated sugar, which dissolves easily and evenly into the batter. Some recipes also include brown sugar, which adds a hint of caramel flavor and helps to create a slightly denser texture. The sugar is typically mixed with the melted butter and chocolate to create a sweet, gooey batter.

Eggs are another important ingredient in brownies. They help to bind the other ingredients together and add moisture to the batter. Most recipes call for large eggs, which provide the right amount of liquid and fat to create a rich, fudgy texture. The eggs are typically beaten and added to the batter one at a time, ensuring that they are fully incorporated.

Flour is the final core ingredient in brownies. It provides structure and stability to the batter. Most recipes call for all-purpose flour, which has a moderate protein content and creates a tender texture. Some recipes also include a small amount of baking powder or baking soda, which helps to create a slightly lighter texture. The flour is typically sifted and added to the batter in small increments, ensuring that it is evenly distributed.

In addition to these core ingredients, there are many variations and additions that can be made to brownie

The Importance of Quality Ingredients for Luxurious Brownies: When it comes to indulging in a decadent treat like brownies, the quality of the ingredients used can make all the difference. Luxurious brownies are not just about the taste, but also about the overall experience of enjoying a rich and satisfying dessert. From the cocoa powder to the butter and sugar, every ingredient plays a crucial role in creating the perfect brownie.

One of the key ingredients in brownies is cocoa powder. High-quality cocoa powder adds a deep and intense chocolate flavor to the brownies. It is important to choose a cocoa powder that is rich in flavor and has a smooth texture. This will ensure that the brownies have a velvety and luscious taste. Using a subpar cocoa powder can result in a bland and lackluster brownie that fails to deliver the desired indulgence.

Another essential ingredient in luxurious brownies is butter. The quality of the butter used can greatly impact the texture and richness of the brownies. Opting for a high-quality butter that is rich in flavor and has a high fat content will result in a moist and tender brownie. Inferior butter can lead to a dry and crumbly texture, taking away from the luxuriousness of the brownie.

Sugar is another ingredient that should not be overlooked when it comes to making luxurious brownies. Using high-quality sugar, such as cane sugar or brown sugar, can enhance the flavor and sweetness of the brownies. These sugars have a more complex flavor profile compared to regular white sugar, adding depth and complexity to the brownies. Additionally, using the right amount of sugar is crucial to achieving the perfect balance of sweetness without overpowering the other flavors.

In addition to these key ingredients, other components such as eggs, flour, and vanilla extract also contribute to the overall quality of the brownies. Using fresh and high-quality eggs will ensure a rich and moist texture. Opting for a good quality flour, such as all-purpose or cake flour, will result in a tender and light brownie. Lastly, using pure vanilla extract instead of artificial flavorings will add a subtle and aromatic note to the brownies.

When it comes to luxurious brownies, every ingredient matters. By using high-quality cocoa powder, butter, sugar, eggs, flour, and vanilla extract, you can elevate your brownie game and create a truly indulgent dessert. The attention to detail and the use of premium ingredients will result in a brownie that is not only delicious but also a luxurious treat

Baking Techniques and Tips for Perfect Brownies Every Time:

Brownies are a beloved dessert that can be enjoyed by people of all ages. Whether you prefer them fudgy or cakey, there are a few baking techniques and tips that can help you achieve perfect brownies every time. From choosing the right ingredients to mastering the baking process, here's a comprehensive guide to baking the best brownies.

1. Choosing the Right Ingredients:

- Cocoa Powder: Opt for high-quality cocoa powder to ensure a rich and intense chocolate flavor in your brownies.

- Chocolate: Use good quality chocolate, either in the form of bars or chips, for a decadent and indulgent taste.

- Butter: Unsalted butter is preferred as it allows you to control the salt content in your brownies.

- Eggs: Use large eggs at room temperature for better incorporation into the batter.

- Sugar: A combination of granulated sugar and brown sugar adds both sweetness and moisture to the brownies.

- Flour: All-purpose flour works well for most brownie recipes, but you can experiment with different types of flour for variations in texture.

2. Mixing the Batter:

- Melt the butter and chocolate together in a heatproof bowl over simmering water or in the microwave, stirring occasionally until smooth.

- In a separate bowl, whisk together the eggs and sugars until well combined.

- Slowly pour the melted chocolate mixture into the egg mixture, whisking continuously to prevent the eggs from scrambling.

- Sift in the flour and cocoa powder, and gently fold them into the wet ingredients until just combined. Overmixing can result in tough brownies.

3. Adding Extra Flavor:

- Vanilla Extract: A teaspoon of vanilla extract enhances the overall flavor of the brownies.

- Nuts: Chopped nuts, such as walnuts or pecans, can add a delightful crunch to your brownies.

- Chocolate Chips: Stir in some chocolate chips into the batter for extra pockets of gooey chocolate.

4. Baking Time and Temperature:

- Preheat your oven to the recommended temperature stated in the recipe.

- Use an oven thermometer to ensure accurate temperature readings.

- Bake the brownies in the center of the oven for the specified time. Avoid opening the oven door too frequently, as it can cause fluctuations in temperature and affect the baking process.

Customizing and Experimenting with Brownie Recipes: Customizing and experimenting with brownie recipes can be a fun and exciting way to add your own personal touch to this classic dessert. Brownies are loved by many for their rich and fudgy texture, and by customizing the recipe, you can create a unique flavor profile that suits your taste preferences.

One way to customize a brownie recipe is by adding different types of chocolate. While traditional brownie recipes call for semi-sweet or dark chocolate, you can experiment with using milk chocolate, white chocolate, or even a combination of different chocolates. Each type of chocolate will bring its own distinct flavor and sweetness to the brownies, allowing you to create a variety of taste experiences.

In addition to experimenting with different types of chocolate, you can also add various mix-ins to your brownie batter. Popular mix-ins include nuts, such as walnuts or pecans, which add a crunchy texture and a nutty flavor to the brownies. You can also try adding dried fruits, like cherries or cranberries, for a burst of sweetness and tanginess. For those who enjoy a bit of indulgence, you can even incorporate chunks of your favorite candy bars or cookies into the batter.

Furthermore, you can customize the texture of your brownies by adjusting the baking time and temperature. If you prefer a gooey and fudgy brownie, you can bake them for a shorter amount of time at a lower temperature. On the other hand, if you prefer a cake-like texture, you can bake them for a longer time at a higher temperature. By experimenting with different baking times and temperatures, you can find the perfect balance between a soft and chewy brownie or a light and fluffy one.

Another way to customize your brownie recipe is by adding different flavorings and spices. For example, you can add a teaspoon of instant coffee or espresso powder to enhance the chocolate flavor. You can also incorporate a teaspoon of vanilla extract or almond extract to add a subtle hint of sweetness. Additionally, spices like cinnamon or chili powder can add a unique and unexpected twist to your brownies.

Finally, you can experiment with different toppings to elevate the presentation and taste of your brownies. A classic option is to dust the top of the brownies with powdered sugar or cocoa powder. You can also drizzle melted chocolate or caramel sauce over the brownies for an extra touch of decadence. For a refreshing twist, you can top your brownies with a scoop of ice cream or a dollop

Techniques for Creating Visually Stunning Brownies:

Brownies are a beloved dessert that can be enjoyed by people of all ages. While the taste and texture of brownies are important, the visual appeal of these treats can also make a significant impact. Creating visually stunning brownies can elevate the overall experience and make them even more enticing to eat. Here are some techniques that can help you achieve this:

1. Swirling Techniques: One way to create visually stunning brownies is by incorporating swirls into the batter. This can be done by adding a contrasting color of batter, such as a chocolate or caramel swirl, to the base brownie batter. Use a toothpick or a skewer to gently swirl the two batters together, creating a marbled effect. This technique not only adds visual interest but also enhances the flavor profile of the brownies.

2. Toppings and Decorations: Another way to make your brownies visually appealing is by adding toppings and decorations. Consider

sprinkling some colorful chocolate chips, nuts, or crushed candies on top of the brownie batter before baking. You can also drizzle melted chocolate or caramel sauce over the baked brownies for an elegant touch. These toppings and decorations not only add visual appeal but also provide additional texture and flavor.

3. Layering: Creating layers in your brownies can add depth and visual interest. For example, you can make a cookie dough layer by spreading a thin layer of cookie dough on the bottom of the baking pan before pouring the brownie batter on top. This creates a delicious contrast between the soft and fudgy brownie layer and the crunchy cookie layer. You can also experiment with layering different flavors of brownie batter, such as chocolate and peanut butter, to create a visually stunning and flavorful treat.

4. Shapes and Sizes: Brownies don't have to be limited to the traditional square or rectangular shape. Using different molds or cookie cutters, you can create brownies in various shapes and sizes. Heart-shaped brownies for Valentine's Day, star-shaped brownies for the Fourth of July, or even bite-sized brownie pops for a party can make your treats visually appealing and fun to eat.

5. Garnishes: Adding garnishes to your brownies can take them to the next level visually. Consider dusting the top of your brownies with powdered sugar or cocoa powder for an elegant touch. You can also garnish them with fresh berries, mint leaves, or edible flowers to add a

Decorating with Ganache, Frosting, and Edible Gold Leaf in Brownies: Decorating with ganache, frosting, and edible gold leaf in brownies is a delightful way to elevate the presentation and taste of this classic dessert. By adding these luxurious elements, you can transform a simple brownie into a decadent and visually stunning treat that is sure to impress your guests.

To begin, let's explore the process of making ganache. Ganache is a rich and velvety mixture of chocolate and cream that can be used as a glaze, filling, or frosting. It adds a luscious and glossy finish to brownies, creating a smooth and indulgent texture. To make ganache, you will need high-quality chocolate and heavy cream. Start by heating the cream in a saucepan until it begins to simmer. Then, pour the hot cream over the chopped chocolate and let it sit for a few minutes to allow the chocolate to melt. Gently stir the mixture until it becomes smooth and shiny. Once the ganache has cooled slightly, you can pour it over the brownies, spreading it evenly with a spatula. The ganache will set as it cools, creating a beautiful and glossy finish.

Next, let's discuss frosting. Frosting is a versatile and delicious way to add flavor and visual appeal to brownies. There are various types of frosting that you can use, such as buttercream, cream cheese, or even a simple powdered sugar glaze. Buttercream frosting is a popular choice as it is creamy, smooth, and can be easily piped or spread onto the brownies. To make buttercream frosting, you will need butter, powdered sugar, vanilla extract, and a pinch of salt. Beat the butter until it becomes light and fluffy, then gradually add the powdered sugar, vanilla extract, and salt. Continue beating until the frosting is smooth and creamy. You can then use a piping bag or a spatula to frost the brownies, creating beautiful swirls or patterns. Cream cheese frosting is another delicious option that adds a tangy and creamy element to the brownies. To make cream cheese frosting, you will need cream cheese, butter, powdered sugar, and vanilla extract. Beat the cream cheese and butter until smooth, then gradually add the powdered sugar and vanilla extract. Beat until the frosting is creamy and spreadable. Spread the cream cheese frosting over the brownies, creating a thick and luscious layer.

Lastly, let's explore the use of edible gold leaf in brownie decoration. Edible gold leaf is

Creative Plating and Presentation Ideas of Brownies:

When it comes to serving brownies, there are countless ways to elevate their presentation and make them even more enticing to your guests. Whether you're hosting a dinner party, a birthday celebration, or simply want to impress your family with a special treat, these creative plating ideas will surely take your brownies to the next level.

1. Decadent Tower: Create a stunning tower of brownies by stacking them on top of each other. Start with a larger brownie as the base and gradually decrease the size as you build upwards. To add a touch of elegance, drizzle some melted chocolate or caramel sauce over the tower and sprinkle it with crushed nuts or colorful sprinkles.

2. Brownie Sundae: Transform your brownies into a delightful sundae by serving them with a scoop of your favorite ice cream. Place a warm brownie at the bottom of a dessert bowl, top it with a generous scoop of ice cream, and drizzle it with hot fudge or caramel sauce. Finish it off with a dollop of whipped cream and a cherry on top.

3. Brownie Parfait: Layer your brownies with a variety of complementary ingredients to create a visually appealing and delicious parfait. Start with a glass or a clear dessert dish and alternate layers of crumbled brownies, whipped cream, fresh berries, and chocolate ganache. Repeat the layers until you reach the top, and garnish with a sprig of mint or a dusting of cocoa powder.

4. Brownie Kabobs: For a fun and interactive dessert option, assemble brownie kabobs. Cut your brownies into bite-sized cubes and thread them onto skewers, alternating with fresh fruits like strawberries, bananas, or pineapple chunks. Serve them on a platter or in a tall glass, and drizzle with melted chocolate for an extra touch of indulgence.

5. Brownie Trifle: Create a show-stopping dessert by layering brownie chunks, chocolate pudding, and whipped cream in a trifle dish. Repeat the layers until you reach the top, and finish with a sprinkle of chocolate shavings or crushed cookies. This dessert not only looks impressive but also allows your guests to enjoy the different textures and flavors in every spoonful.

6. Brownie Tacos: Put a playful twist on traditional brownies by turning them into tacos. Cut your brownies into rectangular shapes and fold them into taco shells.

Pairing Brownies with Complementary Flavors and Textures: When it comes to pairing brownies with complementary flavors and textures, the possibilities are endless. Brownies, with their rich and fudgy texture, provide the perfect canvas for experimenting with different ingredients to enhance their taste and create a harmonious balance of flavors.

One classic pairing that never fails is the combination of brownies with a scoop of creamy vanilla ice cream. The contrast between the warm, gooey brownie and the cold, smooth ice cream creates a delightful sensory experience. The sweetness of the ice cream complements the deep chocolate flavor of the brownie, while the creaminess adds a luxurious touch.

For those who enjoy a bit of crunch in their desserts, adding some chopped nuts to the brownie batter can take the texture to a whole new level. Walnuts, pecans, or almonds provide a satisfying crunch that contrasts beautifully with the softness of the brownie. The nutty flavor also adds an extra dimension to the overall taste.

If you're looking to add a fruity twist to your brownies, consider pairing them with fresh berries. The tartness of berries, such as raspberries or strawberries, cuts through the richness of the brownie and adds a refreshing element. You can either serve the brownies with a side of mixed berries or incorporate them into the batter itself for a burst of fruity flavor in every bite.

For those who enjoy a touch of sophistication, pairing brownies with a drizzle of caramel or a sprinkle of sea salt can elevate the dessert to a whole new level. The sweetness of the caramel complements the chocolatey goodness of the brownie, while the hint of salt adds a subtle savory note that balances out the flavors.

If you're feeling adventurous, you can even experiment with more unconventional pairings. For example, pairing brownies with a hint of spice, such as chili powder or cinnamon, can add an unexpected kick to the dessert. Alternatively, you can try incorporating different types of chocolate, such as white chocolate or dark chocolate chunks, to create a more complex flavor profile.

In conclusion, pairing brownies with complementary flavors and textures opens up a world of possibilities for creating a truly indulgent dessert experience. Whether you prefer classic combinations or want to venture into more unique pairings, there is no shortage of options to explore. So go ahead, get creative, and enjoy the delightful journey of discovering the perfect pairing for your brownies.

Introduction

No matter where in the world you're from, you'll probably love brownies or at least have heard of them. If you don't, we may have just made contact with the aliens...That's how these simple chocolatey treats are loved around the world. The thing is, they're so loved that they've become rather plain and unsurprising. That stops today.

Brownies were never put in this world to be anything less than spectacular, so we've decided to do something about it! Unfortunately, we can't go against the system (is there even one for brownies?) and trash all box mixes everywhere. Thus, we've decided to let the box mixes live for now and concentrate on giving the brownie-lovers of this world what they deserve: a recipe book for exceptional brownies.

What we've come up with is the holy grail of brownies. We've got cream cheese, red velvet, marshmallow, peanut butter, and many more versions of this classic chocolatey treat! Which is why we're expecting you to say goodbye to ordinary brownies as soon as you start on your first recipe. We promise they're amazing! So which are your favorite, gooey or fudgy? We're here to tell you they're both accepted by us, the self-proclaimed Million Dollar Brownie Institute. All you need to do is adjust your baking times to make them gooey or cakey, so just keep an eye on the oven and get ready to bake the brownies of your life.

You won't have any paparazzi chasing you around for making these but your friends, family, and even coworkers will certainly be nagging you to bake a few batches for any and every occasion. Get ready because none of these are one-hit wonders, they'll be your go-to every single time. Good luck!

||||||||||||||||||||||||||||||||||||||||||||||||||||||||||||||||||||||||||||

Recipe 1: Cocoa Tofu Brownies

This recipe features a much healthier version of cocoa brownies. These chocolate goodness are fudgy and super yummy.

Preparation Time: 40 minutes

Portion Size: 12 servings

Ingredient List:

- 3-ounce firm silken tofu
- 1 cup whole wheat flour, divided
- 1/8 tsp. salt
- 1/4 cup brown sugar
- 1/2 tsp. baking powder
- 1 tsp. ground cinnamon
- 1/8 tsp. pumpkin pie spice
- 1/2 cup cocoa powder, unsweetened
- 2 tsp. vanilla extract
- 1/2 cup applesauce, unsweetened

- 3 tbsp. water
- 1/4 cup soy yogurt

||||||||||||||||||||||||||||||||||||||||||||||||||||||||||||||||||||||||||||||

Methods:

Set oven to 325 degrees F and let preheat. Take an 8-inch square baking pan, grease the bottom and inner sides with a non-stick cooking spray and set aside until required. In a bowl place flour, and stir in salt, cinnamon, pumpkin spice, baking powder and cocoa powder. In a food processor or blender, add tofu, yogurt, water and applesauce and blend until smooth. Transfer this mixture into a separate bowl, add sugar and vanilla extract and stir until well mixed. Stir in flour mixture, 2 tbsp. at a time, and spoon this mixture into the prepared pan. Smooth the top using a spatula and place pan into the oven. Bake for 25 minutes or until done and inserted a wooden skewer into the pan comes out clean. Let brownies cool in pan for 15 minutes in the pan before turning out to cool completely. Cut into 12 squares and serve.

Recipe 2: Hazelnut Brownies

Hazelnut brownies are one of the best chocolate brownies that are moist, buttery, and extremely delicious. These nutty treats are perfect gifts to your friends and special people.

Preparation Time:50 minutes

Portion Size:20 servings

Ingredient List:

- 1 3/4 cups all-purpose flour, leveled
- 1 tsp. salt
- 2 1/2 cups brown sugar
- 1 tsp. baking powder
- 3 tbsp. cocoa powder
- 6 ounce chopped chocolate, unsweetened
- 1 1/4 cup hazelnuts
- 1 cup unsalted butter
- 1 cup water

- 2 tsp. vanilla extract
- 5 eggs

||||||||||||||||||||||||||||||||||||||||||||||||||||||||||||||||||||||||||||||

Methods:

Set oven to 350 degrees F and let preheat. Take a 9-inch square baking pan, line with parchment sheet and set aside until required. Place a small saucepan over medium-low heat, add butter, sugar, and water and bring the mixture to simmer. Then, remove the pan from the heat and whisk in chocolate until combined. Using an electric beater beat in eggs and vanilla at high speed until fluffy. Stir in flour mixture, 2 tbsp. at a time, until incorporated and then fold in hazelnuts. Spoon the mixture into the baking pan and bake for 40 minutes or until inserted wooden skewer into the center of pan has come out clean. Let the brownie cool for 10 minutes before turning out onto a wire rack to cool completely. Cut into squares and serve.

Recipe 3: Chocolate Brownie

These chocolate brownies are fudgy in taste, gooey from inside and crackly from outside. Make a large bunch and have it any time of the day.

Preparation Time:60 minutes

Portion Size:16 servings

Ingredient List:

- 3/4 cup and 2 tbsp. all-purpose flour
- 7 ounces chopped chocolate, unsweetened
- 1/2 tsp. salt
- 1 cup white sugar
- 1 cup brown sugar
- 1/4 tsp. baking powder
- 3 eggs

- 7 tbsp. unsalted butter and more for greasing
- 3 tbsp. coconut oil

||||||||||||||||||||||||||||||||||||||||||||||||||||||||||||||||||||||||||||||||||||

Methods:

Set oven to 350 degrees F and let it preheat. Take a 9-inch square pan, grease the bottom and inner sides with butter. Line greased the pan with parchment sheet, leaving 2-inch of the sheet hanging from the sides, set aside until used. In a microwave ovenproof bowl place chocolate, add butter and coconut oil and let microwave for 45 to 60 seconds or until chocolate is melt completely, stirring after 30 seconds. Into melted chocolate, using an electric beater beat in the egg for 1 minute or until smooth. Place flour in a separate medium-sized bowl, add salt and baking powder and whisk until mixed well. Stir this mixture into chocolate mixture, 2 tbsp. at a time, until incorporated. Spoon batter into the prepared baking pan and smooth the top using a spatula. Place pan into the oven and bake for 35 to 40 minutes or until inserted wooden skewer into the center of pan comes out with moist crumbs. Let the brownie cool on wire rack completely, then cut into squares and serve.

Recipe 4: Blueberry Brownies

Blueberry brownies are amazingly delicious and intensely fudgy. It is vegan and extremely nutritious.

Preparation Time:55 minutes

Portion Size:12 servings

Ingredient List:

- 1 cup blueberries, fresh
- 1 1/2 cups all-purpose flour
- ## 1 1/4 cups chocolate chips, semi-sweet
- 1/4 tsp. salt
- 3/4 cup brown sugar
- 1/4 tsp. baking powder
- 1/2 tsp. baking soda
- 1/4 cup cocoa powder, unsweetened
- ## 10-ounce blueberry preserves

- 2 tsp. vanilla extract
- 1/2 tsp. almond extract
- 1/2 cup olive oil
- 1/4 cup soy milk

||||||||||||||||||||||||||||||||||||||||||||||||||||||||||||||||||||||||||||||

Methods:

Set oven to 325 degrees F and let preheat. Take a 9 by 13-inch baking pan, grease the bottom and inner sides with a non-stick cooking spray and set aside until required. In a microwave ovenproof bowl place 2/3 cups chocolate chips and microwave for 30 to 45 seconds or until melt, stirring after 30 seconds. In another bowl place sugar, oil, almond and vanilla extract, oil and blueberry preserve. Blend at high speed for 2 to 3 minutes or until smooth. Then stir in flour, 2 tbsp. at a time, salt, baking soda, baking powder and salt until mixed. Stir in melted chocolate and then fold in chocolate chips and blueberries until just mix. Spoon the mixture into your prepared pan and then smooth the top using the spatula. Place pan into the oven and bake for about 45 minutes or until done and until inserted wooden skewer into the center of pan comes out clean. Let the brownie cool in pan for 15 minutes before turning out to cool completely on wire rack. Cut into wedges and serve.

Recipe 5: Cherry Pecan Brownies

Give a decadent twist to the pecan brownie by pairing it with cherries. It's the ultimate chocolate lover's brownie.

Preparation Time:45 minutes

Portion Size:20 servings

Ingredient List:

- 4-ounce plain flour
- 7-ounce unsalted butter, and more for greasing pan
- 6-ounce brown sugar
- 6-ounce caster sugar
- 2-ounce cocoa powder, unsweetened
- 4-ounce plain dark chocolate
- 4-ounce white chocolate
- 4-ounce shelled pecan, halved
- 3-ounce dried sour cherries
- 4 eggs

Methods:

Set oven to 350 degrees F and let preheat. Take an 8-inch square baking pan, grease with butter. Line the greased pan with parchment sheet, leaving 2-inch of the sheet hanging from the sides, set aside until required. Place a medium-sized saucepan over low heat, add butter and let heat for 2 to 3 minutes or until butter melt completely. Then, remove from the heat, add in sugar, and whisk until mixed well. In a separate bowl place eggs and whisk until smooth. Slowly whisk in butter mixture until well combined. Add in cocoa powder and flour, 2 tbsp. at a time, until incorporated. Let mixture rest for 10 minutes. In the meantime, cut chocolate into 3/4-inch pieces and fold into cooled brownie batter along with pecans and cherries until just mix. Spoon the mixture into the pan and smooth the top using a spatula. Place pan into the oven and bake for 25 - 30 minutes or until inserted wooden skewer into the center of pan comes out with moist crumbs. Let the brownie cool in pan for 15 minutes before turning it out. Cut into squares and serve.

Recipe 6: Dark-Chocolate Spelt Brownies

This dessert is a perfect way to use spelt brownie to prepare a deliciously sweet treat. This chocolaty goodness is scrumptiously rich and chewy.

Preparation Time: 120 minutes

Portion Size: 16 servings

Ingredient List:

- 3/4 cup spelt flour
- 6-ounce bittersweet chocolate, chopped
- 1/4 cup cocoa powder, unsweetened
- 1/2 tsp. salt
- 3/4 cup white sugar
- 3/4 cup brown sugar

- 3 eggs
- 4-ounce grated unsalted butter, and more for greasing pan

|||||||||||||||||||||||||||||||||||||||||||||||||||||||||||||||||||||||||||||

Methods:

Set oven to 350 degrees F and let it preheat. Take an 8-inch square pan, grease the bottom and inner sides with butter. Line greased the pan with parchment sheet, leaving 2-inch of the sheet hanging from the sides, set aside until required. In a microwave ovenproof bowl place chocolate and butter and let microwave for 45 to 60 seconds or until chocolate is melt completely, stirring after 30 seconds. Into melted chocolate, using an electric beater whisk in eggs, one at a time, until combined. Then whisk in salt and cocoa and fold in flour, 2 tbsp. at a time, until incorporated. Spoon the mixture into the prepared pan and smooth the top with a spatula. Place pan into the oven and bake for 35 to 40 minutes or until inserted wooden skewer into the center and it comes out with moist crumbs. Let the brownie cool on wire rack completely, then cut into squares and serve.

Recipe 7: Dark and White Chocolate Cherry Brownies

These easy-to-make brownies feature chocolate and the fruity flavor of cherries. Serve this decadent dessert on Christmas dinners.

Preparation Time:40 minutes

Portion Size:12 servings

Ingredient List:

- 6-ounce fresh cherries, cored and halved
- 4-ounce all-purpose flour, leveled
- 9-ounce brown sugar
- 1 tsp. baking powder
- 12-ounce grated chocolate
- 6-ounce white chocolate, chopped
- 2 tbsp. cocoa powder, unsweetened
- 9-ounce unsalted butter, and more for greasing pan

- 3 eggs

||||||||||||||||||||||||||||||||||||||||||||||||||||||||||||||||||||||||||||||||||

Methods:

Set oven to 350 degrees F and let preheat. Take an 8-inch square baking pan, grease with butter. Line the greased pan with parchment sheet, leaving 2-inch of the sheet hanging from the sides, set aside until required. Place a medium-sized saucepan over medium-low heat, add butter and chocolate and let heat for 5 minutes or until chocolate melt completely, stirring frequently. In the meantime, place sugar in a bowl, add sugar and beat using an electric beat until creamy. Cool melted chocolate mixture and add into eggs mixture and whisk until combined. Then fold in flour, 2 tbsp. at a time, baking powder and half of the cherries or until just mixed. Spoon this mixture into the prepared pan and top with white chocolate and remaining cherry halves. Place pan in the oven and bake for 25 to 30 minutes or until inserted wooden skewer in the center of pan comes out with moist crumbs. Let the brownie cool in pan for 10 minutes. Then, sprinkle cocoa powder across the top, cut into squares and serve.

Recipe 8: Cookies and Cream Brownies

One word for these brownies, EPIC! These rich and fudgy brownies make this recipe is a perfect way to use leftover cookies.

Preparation Time: 50 minutes

Portion Size: 16 servings

Ingredient List:

- 2 tbsp. plain flour
- 1/8 tsp. salt
- 6-ounce brown sugar
- 1 tbsp. cocoa powder, unsweetened
- 6 ounce grated dark chocolate, unsweetened
- 6-ounce chocolate biscuits, quartered
- 2 tsp. vanilla extract
- 6-ounce unsalted butter and more for greasing pan
- 3 eggs

- 2 egg yolks

||||||||||||||||||||||||||||||||||||||||||||||||||||||||||||||||||||||||||||||||||

Methods:

Set oven to 350 degrees F and let preheat. Take an 8-inch square baking pan, grease with butter. Line the greased pan with parchment sheet, leaving 2-inch of the sheet hanging from the sides, set aside until required. Place a small saucepan over medium-low heat, add butter and let heat for 2 to 3 minutes or until melt completely. Then, remove the pan from the heat, add chocolate and whisk for 2 minutes or until chocolate melt completely. In a separate bowl place vanilla, eggs and egg yolks and using an electric beater, beat until fluffy. Gradually beat in sugar until well-combined and mixture becomes stiffer. Beat in the prepared chocolate mixture, flour, salt and cocoa until incorporated. Fold in a third portion of chocolate pieces and spoon the mixture into the prepared pan. Smooth the top using a spatula, scatter remaining chocolate biscuits pieces across the top and press slightly in the batter. Place pan in the middle baking rack of the oven and bake for 25 to 30 minutes or until inserted wooden skewer into the center of pan comes out with moist crumbs. Let the brownie cool in pan completely, then cut into squares and serve.

Recipe 9: Chocolate & Walnut Brownies

Add crunch and nutty taste to a chocolate brownie by adding walnuts. Feel free to use your favorite nuts in the recipe.

Preparation Time:30 minutes

Portion Size:16 servings

Ingredient List:

- 2/3 cup almond flour
- 1/4 tsp. salt
- 1/3 cup brown sugar
- 1/2 tsp. baking soda
- 8 ounces dark chocolate, chopped
- 2 tbsp. cocoa powder, unsweetened
- 1/2 cup chopped walnuts
- 1/3 cup maple syrup

- 2 eggs
- 1/3 cup olive oil, and more for greasing the pan

||||||||||||||||||||||||||||||||||||||||||||||||||||||||||||||||||||||||||||||||

Methods:

Set oven to 350 degrees F and let preheat. Take an 8-inch square pan and line greased the pan with parchment sheet, leaving 2-inch of the sheet hanging from the sides. Grease the bottom and inner sides with oil and set pan aside until required. Place a small saucepan over medium-low heat, add half of the chocolate and let heat until chocolate is melt completely, stirring after 30 seconds. Into melted chocolate, using an electric beater whisk in sugar, maple syrup, and oil until combined. Remove pan from the heat and beat in eggs, one at a time, and then beat in salt, baking soda, and cocoa powder until mixed. Stir in remaining chocolate and flour, 2 tbsp. at a time, until incorporated. Spoon this mixture into the prepared pan and smooth the top using a spatula. Sprinkle walnuts over the top and place pan into the oven. Bake for 30 minutes or until inserted wooden skewer into the center of pan comes out clean. Let the brownie cool in pan for 10 minutes then turn out on a wire rack to cool completely. Cut into squares and serve.

Recipe 10: Peanut Butter Brownies

Every bite of these gooey brownies features chocolate chips and peanut butter. This incredible dessert is always a hit at family and friends' parties.

Preparation Time:75 minutes

Portion Size:12 servings

Ingredient List:

- 1/4 cup and 2 tbsp. almond flour
- 1/8 tsp. salt
- 2/3 cup brown sugar
- 1 1/2 tsp. baking soda
- 1 tsp. vanilla extract
- 1/4 cup chocolate chips, unsweetened
- # 1 cup peanut butter
- 1/4 cup applesauce

- 2 tbsp. almond milk

||||||||||||||||||||||||||||||||||||||||||||||||||||||||||||||||||||||||||||||||||||

Methods:

Set oven to 350 degrees F and let preheat. Take an 8-inch square baking pan, grease the bottom and inner sides with a non-stick cooking spray and set aside until required. In a bowl place flour, and add salt, sugar, baking soda and chocolate chips. Stir until mixed. In another bowl place vanilla, peanut butter, apple sauce and milk and stir until combined. Stir in flour mixture, 2 tbsp. at a time, until incorporated. Spoon the batter into the prepared pan and smooth the top using a spatula. Sprinkle chocolate chips over the top and place pan into the oven. Bake for 10 minutes or until done and the top layer is set. Let brownie rest for 45 minutes in the pan or until firm. Then, cut into 12 squares and serve.

Recipe 11: Irish Coffee Brownies

The coffee addicts will love this delicious dessert. Prepare a large batch and nibble on this decadent treat any time of the day.

Preparation Time: 2 hours and 45 minutes

Portion Size: 24 servings

Ingredient List:

- 2 cups brown sugar
- 2 cups all-purpose flour, leveled
- 1 tsp. salt
- 3/4 cup confectioners' sugar, sifted
- 1 tsp. baking powder
- 1/4 tsp. baking soda
- 3 tbsp. ground coffee
- 1 cup unsalted butter, and more for greasing pan

- 1 tbsp. melted butter, warm
- 2 eggs
- 2 tbsp. Irish whiskey
- 1 tsp. vanilla extract
- 1/2 cup sliced almonds

||||||||||||||||||||||||||||||||||||||||||||||||||||||||||||||||||||||||||||

Methods:

Set oven to 350 degrees F and let preheat. Take a 9 by 13-inch baking pan, line with parchment sheet, leaving 2-inch of the sheet hanging from the sides. Place a small saucepan over medium-low heat, add butter and let heat until melt completely. Transfer into a large bowl, add salt, sugar, and coffee and whisk until combined. Using an electric beater, beat in eggs and vanilla at high speed until fluffy. In separate bowl place flour, add baking powder and baking soda and stir until mixed well. Stir this mixture into the egg mixture, 2 tbsp. at a time, until incorporated. Spoon this mixture into your prepared pan, smooth the top using a spatula and then sprinkle almonds over the top. Place pan into the oven and bake for 30 minutes or until inserted wooden skewer into the center of pan has come out clean. In the meantime, whisk together melted butter and whiskey until combined. Then, gradually whisk in confectioners' sugar until thick mixture forms. Let the brownie cool in pan for 10 minutes before turning out to cool completely on a wire rack and then cut into squares. Place prepared butter-whiskey mixture into a piping bag and drizzle over brownies. Let brownies rest for 1 hour or until top is dry and serve.

Recipe 12: White Chocolate Chili Brownie

The combination of white chocolate and chilies makes a devilish tasty brownie. Serve them warm.

Preparation Time: 50 minutes

Portion Size: 24 servings

Ingredient List:

- 1 large red chili pepper, cored and sliced diagonally
- 1 large green chili pepper, cored and sliced diagonally
- 7-ounce plain flour, leveled
- 1/8 tsp. salt
- 1 cup caster sugar, divided
- 10-ounce white chocolate, chopped
- 7-ounce unsalted butter and more for greasing pan
- 1/2 tsp. vanilla extract
- 3 eggs

- 5 fluid ounce water

||||||||||||||||||||||||||||||||||||||||||||||||||||||||||||||||||||||||||||||||

Methods:

Set oven to 350 degrees F and let preheat. Take a 9-inch square baking pan, grease with butter. Line the greased pan with parchment sheet, leaving 2-inch of the sheet hanging from the sides, set aside until required. Place a small saucepan over medium heat, add chilies, water, and 3-ounce sugar and bring the mixture to boil, and then simmer for 5 minutes. In the meantime, place half of the white chocolate in a microwave ovenproof bowl, add butter and microwave for 45 to 60 seconds or until chocolate melt completely, stirring after 30 seconds. Let melted chocolate cool. Place eggs in a separate bowl, add remaining sugar and vanilla and beat using an electric beater beat until fluffy. Then beat in white chocolate mixture and stir in salt and flour, 2 tbsp. at a time, or until incorporated. Drain chilies and fold the third portion into the batter. Spoon the mixture into the prepared pan and sprinkle remaining chilies across the top. Bake for 25 to 30 minutes or until inserted wooden skewer into the center of pan comes out with moist crumbs. Let the brownie cool in pan completely, then cut into squares and serve.

Recipe 13: Cream Cheese Brownies

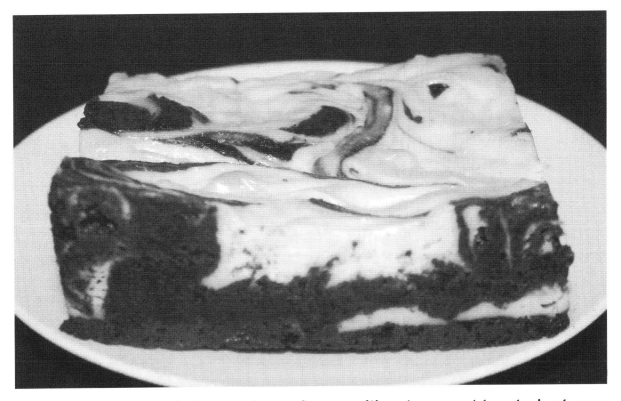

Cream cheese and chocolate make an ultimate sweet treat. Just pop the brownie batter into a slow cooker and see the magic happens.

Preparation Time: 2 hours and 15 minutes

Portion Size: 24 servings

Ingredient List:

- 3-ounce all-purpose flour, leveled
- 3-ounce chocolate, unsweetened
- 10-ounce caster sugar
- 4-ounce grated butter
- 3 cups cream cheese, softened
- 1 tsp. vanilla extract
- # 1 tbsp. condensed milk
- 2 eggs

Methods:

Take a 5-quarts slow cooker, line with parchment sheet and set aside until required. In a microwave ovenproof bowl place chocolate and butter and microwave for 45 to 60 seconds or until melt completely, stirring after 30 seconds. Into melted chocolate beat in sugar until combined. Then stir in vanilla and fold in flour, 2 tbsp. at a time, until incorporated. Spoon this mixture into the prepared slow cooker and smooth the top with a spatula. In a bowl place cream cheese and condensed milk and whisk until just mix. Drizzle this mixture over brownie batter in the slow cooker and make a swirl using a fork or wooden toothpick, don't over mix. Cover slow cooker with lid and switch on. Cook for 2 ½ hours at high heat setting or until inserted wooden skewer into the center of the cooker comes out clean. Cool brownie on a wire rack completely, then cut into squares and serve.

Recipe 14: Black and White Brownies

With this recipe, you won't be able to stop eating these brownies with the taste of cream cheese on top.

Preparation Time:50 minutes

Portion Size:20 servings

Ingredient List:

- 1 3/4 cups all-purpose flour, leveled
- 1 tsp. salt
- 2 1/2 cups brown sugar
- 1 1/2 cup confectioners' sugar
- 1 tsp. baking powder
- 3 tbsp. cocoa powder
- 6 ounce chopped chocolate, unsweetened
- 3 tsp. vanilla extract
- 1 1/2 cup unsalted butter
- 8-ounce cream cheese, soften
- 1 cup water

- 5 eggs

||||||||||||||||||||||||||||||||||||||||||||||||||||||||||||||||||||||||||||

Methods:

Set oven to 350 degrees F and let preheat. Take a 9-inch square baking pan, line with parchment sheet and set aside until required. Place a small saucepan over medium-low heat, add 1 cup butter, sugar and water and bring the mixture to simmer. Then remove the pan from the heat and whisk in chocolate until combined. Using an electric beater beat in eggs and 2 tsp. vanilla at high speed until fluffy. Stir in flour mixture, 2 tbsp. at a time, until incorporated and then fold in hazelnuts. Spoon the mixture into the prepared pan and bake for 35 minutes or until inserted wooden skewer into the center of pan comes out clean. In the meantime, place cream cheese in a bowl and add confectioners' sugar, remaining butter and vanilla and beat at high speed until combined. Let the brownie cool in the pan for 10 minutes before turning out to cool completely. Cut in squares, topped with a heaping tbsp. of cream cheese mixture and serve.

Recipe 15: Triple Chocolate Brownies

Use your slow cooker for preparing this rich and decadent dessert. It is incredibly moist and fudgy.

Preparation Time:3 hours and 45 minutes

Portion Size:14 servings

Ingredient List:

- 1 cups all-purpose flour, leveled
- 1/2 tsp. salt
- # 1 cup white sugar
- 3/4 tsp. baking powder
- 1/4 cup cocoa powder, unsweetened
- 8 ounces bittersweet chocolate, chopped
- # 1 cup chopped walnut
- # 1 cup chocolate chips, semi sweet

- 1/2 cup grated butter, unsalted
- 3 eggs

||||||||||||||||||||||||||||||||||||||||||||||||||||||||||||||||||||||||||||

Methods:

Take a 5-quarts slow cooker, grease the bottom and inner sides with a non-stick cooking spray. Line the bottom of the cooker with a parchment sheet and set aside until used. In a microwave ovenproof bowl place chocolate and butter and microwave for 45 to 60 seconds or until chocolate melt completely, stirring after 30 seconds. Using an electric beater beat in sugar and eggs at high speed until fluffy. Place flour in a separate bowl, add salt, baking powder, and cocoa and stir until combined. Then beat in flour mixture at slow speed into the egg mixture, along with chocolate chips and walnuts until incorporated, don't over mix. Spoon this mixture into the prepared slow cooker and cover with lid. Switch on slow cooker and cook for 3 1/2 hours at high heat setting until done. Let brownies cool on a wire rack completely before cutting into squares. Serve.

Recipe 16: Flourless Applesauce Brownies

This flourless, butterless and sugar-free brownie needs only three pantry ingredients to come together. This brownie is suitable for every type of lifestyle, be it vegan, keto, gluten-free, paleo or keto.

Preparation Time:50 minutes

Portion Size:6 servings

Ingredient List:

- 2/3 cup cocoa powder
- 1/2 cup almond butter
- 8 fluid ounce applesauce, unsweetened

||||||||||||||||||||||||||||||||||||||||||||||||||||||||||||||||||||||||||||||||

Methods:

Set oven to 350 degrees F and let preheat. In the meantime, take a 4 by 6-inch loaf pan, grease the bottom and sides with a non-stick cooking spray and then set aside until required. In a large bowl, place butter and apple sauce and using an electric beater beat at high speed or until combined and smooth. Add cocoa powder and stir until incorporated and a thick batter comes together. Spoon this mixture into the prepared loaf pan and place pan into the oven. Bake for 35 to 40 minutes or until inserted wooden skewer into the center of the loaf comes out clean. Let baked loaf cool for 15 minutes and transfer to a wire rack to let it cool completely. Then cut into 6 wedges and serve.

Recipe 17: Whole-Wheat Brownies

Give ordinary brownies a healthy boost by preparing them using whole-wheat flour and apple sauce. They are fudgy and very nice.

Preparation Time: 30 minutes

Portion Size: 16 servings

Ingredient List:

- 1/2 cup all-purpose flour, leveled
- 1/2 cup whole-wheat flour, leveled
- 1 tsp. salt
- 1 cup brown sugar
- 1 1/4 tsp. baking powder
- 1/4 tsp. baking soda
- 1/3 cup cocoa powder, unsweetened
- 8 ounces semisweet chocolate, chopped

- 6 tbsp. unsalted butter, melted and more for greasing
- 1 1/4 cups applesauce, unsweetened
- 1 egg

||||||||||||||||||||||||||||||||||||||||||||||||||||||||||||||||||||||||||

Methods:

Set oven to 350 degrees F and let preheat. Take an 8-inch square baking pan, grease with butter. Line the greased pan with parchment sheet, leaving 2-inch of the sheet hanging from the sides, set aside until required. In a microwave ovenproof bowl place butter and 6-ounce chocolate and microwave for 45 to 60 seconds or until chocolate melt completely, stirring after 30 seconds. In the meantime, in a large bowl beat together brown sugar, applesauce, and egg until combined. Add melted chocolate mixture and stir until mixed well. In a separate bowl stir together salt, flours, baking powder, baking soda and cocoa until mixed. Add this mixture into chocolate mixture, 2 tbsp. at a time, until incorporated. Spoon this mixture into the prepared pan, sprinkle remaining chocolate across the top and place pan in the oven. Bake for 40 minutes or until inserted wooden skewer into the center of pan comes out clean. Let the brownie cool in pan for 10 minutes before turning out to cool completely on a wire rack. Cut into squares and serve.

Recipe 18: Fudgy Cocoa Brownies

Fudgy cocoa brownies fit perfectly as a classic dessert that is not only delicious but also healthy. The taste is way better than those factory-made in the package.

Preparation Time:35 minutes

Portion Size:12 servings

Ingredient List:

- 2/3 cup sweet potato puree
- 1/2 cup whole-wheat pastry flour
- 1/4 tsp. salt
- 1 cup white sugar
- 1/4 tsp. baking powder
- 2/3 cup cocoa powder, unsweetened
- 1/4 tsp. instant coffee powder

- 4 tbsp. unsalted butter
- 1 1/2 tsp. vanilla extract
- 1 egg

||||||||||||||||||||||||||||||||||||||||||||||||||||||||||||||||||||||||||||||

Methods:

Set oven to 350 degrees F and let preheat. Take an 8-inch square-shaped baking pan, grease the bottom and inner sides with butter and set aside until required. Place a medium sized saucepan over low heat, add butter and let heat until melt completely. Then, remove the pan from the heat, whisk in cocoa powder and let cool slightly. In a separate bowl whisk together sweet potato puree, sugar, and egg until combined and then add to cocoa mixture. Take a small bowl and add flour in it. Add salt and baking powder and stir until just mix. Stir this mixture into cocoa mixture, 2 tbsp. at a time, until incorporated. Spoon this mixture into the prepared pan and smooth the top using a spatula. Bake for 20 to 25 minutes or until inserted wooden skewer into the center of pan comes out with moist crumbs. Cool brownie on a wire rack, then cut into squares to serve.

Recipe 19: Chocolate and Raspberry Brownies

This brownie recipe features the combination of the wonderfully rich flavor of chocolate and the sweetness of raspberries. You can serve this quick-to-fix brownie any time of the day.

Preparation Time: 60 minutes

Portion Size: 16 servings

Ingredient List:

- 6-ounce fresh raspberries
- 4-ounce plain flour, leveled
- 1/8 tsp. salt
- 9-ounce brown sugar
- 1 tsp. baking powder
- 12-ounce dark chocolate
- 9-ounce unsalted butter and more for greasing pan

- 3 eggs

||||||||||||||||||||||||||||||||||||||||||||||||||||||||||||||||||||||||||||||

Methods:

Set oven to 350 degrees F and let preheat. Take a 9-inch square baking pan, grease with butter. Line the greased pan with parchment sheet, leaving 2-inch of the sheet hanging from the sides, set aside until required. Place a medium-sized saucepan over medium-low heat, add butter and chocolate and let heat for 5 minutes or until chocolate melt completely, stirring frequently. In the meantime, in a bowl using an electric beater beat together eggs until fluffy. Then beat in sugar and chocolate mixture until combined. Stir in baking powder, salt, and flour, 2 tbsp. at a time, or until incorporated. Spoon half of the batter in to the prepared pan and layer with berries. Then cover with remaining brownie batter and smooth the top with a spatula. Place pan in the oven and then bake for 40 minutes or until inserted wooden skewer into the center and it comes out with moist crumbs. Let the brownie cool in pan for 10 minutes before turning out to completely on wire rack. Cut into squares and serve.

Recipe 20: Banana Split Pudding Brownies

This recipe is great to make something amazing with bananas. The combination of fudgy brownie and banana pudding forms an unbelievable gooey and heavenly dessert.

Preparation Time: 40 minutes

Portion Size: 12 servings

Ingredient List:

- 1 1/2 cups mashed banana, divided
- 3/4 cup all-purpose flour
- 1/4 cup cocoa powder
- 1/8 tsp. salt
- 1 cup and 2 tbsp. white sugar, divided
- 1/4 tsp. baking soda
- 1 tbsp. arrowroot

- 4 ounces semisweet chocolate, chopped
- 1/3 cup melted coconut oil
- 1 1/2 tsp. vanilla extract, divided
- 1/4 cup soymilk

||||||||||||||||||||||||||||||||||||||||||||||||||||||||||||||||||||||||||||||

Methods:

Set oven to 350 degrees F and let preheat. Place a 9 by 13-inch baking pan, grease the bottom and sides with a non-stick cooking spray and set aside until required. Place semi-sweet chocolate chips in a microwave ovenproof bowl and microwave for 30 to 45 seconds or until melt, stir after 30 seconds. In a bowl add flour and mix in salt, baking soda, and cocoa powder. In another large bowl place 1 cup mashed banana and add 1 cup sugar and oil, stir until mixed well. Whisk in 1 tsp. vanilla and melted chocolate, and then using a hand beater, stir in flour mixture, 2 tbsp. at a time, or until incorporated. Spoon this mixture into the prepared pan and smooth the top using the spatula. In a separate stir together remaining of each banana, sugar and vanilla, soy milk and arrow root. Evenly spread this mixture over brownie batter and place pan into the oven. Let bake for 30 minutes or until done and inserted a wooden skewer into the center of pan comes out clean. Let the brownie cool in pan for 15 minutes before turning out to cool completely. Cut into 12 squares and serve.

Recipe 21: Pecan Brownies

Irresistible pecan brownies are rich and easy to make dessert. This decadent sweet needs ordinary kitchen items to come together.

Preparation Time: 50 minutes

Portion Size: 16 servings

Ingredient List:

- 1/4 cup cocoa powder, unsweetened
- 12 ounces chocolate chips, semi sweet
- 1/2 tsp. salt
- 3/4 cup white sugar
- 1/2 tsp. ground cinnamon
- 1/3 cup cornstarch
- 6 tbsp. grated unsalted butter, and more for greasing pan
- 1 tsp. vanilla extract
- 3 eggs
- 1 cup chopped toasted pecans

||||||||||||||||||||||||||||||||||||||||||||||||||||||||||||||||||||||||||||||

Methods:

Set oven to 350 degrees F and let preheat. Take an 8-inch square baking pan, grease with butter. Line the greased pan with parchment sheet, leaving 2-inch of the sheet hanging from the sides, set aside until required. In a large microwave ovenproof bowl place butter and chocolate and microwave for 45 to 60 seconds or until melt completely, stirring after 30 seconds. Into melted butter-chocolate mixture, whisk in vanilla and sugar until combined. Using an electric beater beat in eggs until fluffy. In a separate bowl stir together cocoa, cinnamon, and cocoa until mix. Then stir this mixture into egg mixture, 2 tbsp. at a time, or until incorporated. Fold in pecans and spoon this mixture into prepared pan. Smooth the top using a spatula and place pan into the oven. Bake for 35 minutes or until inserted wooden skewer into the center of pan comes out clean. Let the brownie cool in pan for 10 minutes before turning out to cool completely. Cut into square and serve.

Recipe 22: Black Bean Avocado Brownies

Make brownies with black beans and avocado, instead of flour and butter. Everyone will love this gluten-free and vegan chocolaty goodness.

Preparation Time: 45 minutes

Portion Size: 12 servings

Ingredient List:

- Half of a medium-sized avocado
- 15 ounce cooked black beans
- 1 tbsp. ground flaxseed
- 1/4 tsp. baking soda
- 1/4 tsp. baking powder
- 2/3 cup cocoa powder, unsweetened
- 1/2 cup brown sugar
- 3 tbsp. water
- 1 tbsp. vanilla extract

- 1 tsp. coconut oil
- 1/3 cup and 2 tbsp. vegan chocolate chips

||||||||||||||||||||||||||||||||||||||||||||||||||||||||||||||||||||||||||||||

Methods:

In a small bowl stir together flax seeds and water until combined and let rest for 5 minutes. Set oven to 350 degrees F and let preheat. Take an 8-inch square baking pan, grease the bottom and sides with a non-stick baking pan and set aside until required. In a food processor place flax seeds mixture, add beans, avocado, sugar and vanilla extract, and pulse until smooth. Add cocoa powder, baking soda, baking powder, coconut oil and continue blending until thick batter comes together Fold in 3/4 cup chocolate chips and transfer into a mixture to a prepared baking pan. Smooth the top using a spatula, then sprinkle remaining chocolate chips over the top and place pan into the oven. Bake for 30 minutes or until inserted wooden skewer into the center of pan comes out clean. Let brownie rest in pan for 15 minutes before turning out to cool completely on wire rack. Then cut into 12 wedges and serve.

Recipe 23: Vegan Brownies

This vegan treat is decadent and incredibly rich. Serve these brownies as a dessert or treat guests at Christmas dinner.

Preparation Time:60 minutes

Portion Size:12 servings

Ingredient List:

- 3-ounce glacé cherry, rinsed and halved
- 4.5-ounce self-raising flour
- 2 tbsp. ground flaxseed
- 4 tbsp. cocoa powder, unsweetened
- 1/2 tsp. coffee granules
- 4-ounce dark chocolate
- 1/4 tsp. baking powder

- 8-ounce caster sugar
- 2.5-ounce ground almond
- 3-ounce cashew butter, and more for greasing pan
- 1 1/2 tsp. vanilla extract
- 6 tbsp. water

|||||||||||||||||||||||||||||||||||||||||||||||||||||||||||||||||||||||

Methods:

Set oven to 300 degrees F and let preheat. Take an 8-inch square baking pan, line with parchment sheet and set aside until required. In a small bowl place flaxseed, add water, stir until just mix and let rest for 5 minutes. Meantime, place a medium-sized saucepan over low heat, add coffee granule, chocolate, and butter and let heat for 2 to 3 minutes or until chocolate melts completely, stirring frequently. Then, remove the pan from the heat and let cool slightly. In a large bowl place flour, cocoa powder, baking powder, 1/4 tsp. salt and stir until well mixed. Transfer melted chocolate mixture into a bowl, add sugar and whisk until sugar dissolves completely. Stir in flour mixture, 2 tbsp. at a time, then vanilla and cherries until a thick dough come together. Spoon this mixture into the prepared baking pan, smooth the top with spatula and place pan into the oven. Bake for 45 minutes or until done and inserted a wooden skewer into the center of the pan comes out clean. Let the brownie cool in pan for 15 minutes before turning out to cool completely. Then, cut in 12 square pieces and serve.

Recipe 24: Honey Brownies

Impress your guests on family get-together events with this unique dessert, featuring an awesome combination of honey and chocolate. Feel free to use any variety of honey.

Preparation Time: 2 hours and 15 minutes

Portion Size: 16 servings

Ingredient List:

- 4-ounce unsalted butter, and more for greasing pan
- 1 1/4 cups all-purpose flour
- 1/3 cup honey
- 3/4 cup brown sugar
- 1 egg
- 2 tsp. vanilla extract
- 1 tsp. salt
- 4 ounces grated bittersweet chocolate

Methods:

Set your oven to 350 degrees F and let preheat. Take an 8-inch square pan, grease the bottom and inner sides with butter. Line greased the pan with parchment sheet, leaving 2-inch of the sheet hanging from the sides, set aside until required. Place a small saucepan over medium heat, add butter and honey and let heat until butter melt completely. Then stir in sugar and transfer this mixture into a bowl. Immediately whisk in egg and then stir in salt and flour, 2 tbsp. at a time, until incorporated. Let mixture cool for 30 minutes and then fold in chocolate. Spoon the mixture into the prepared pan and smooth the top using a spatula. Place pan into the oven and bake for 30 minutes or until inserted wooden skewer into the center and it has come out clean. Then let it cool for 10 minutes before turning out to completely cool on a wire rack. Cut into squares and serve.

Recipe 25: Chocolate & Cherry Brownies

These fruity chocolate brownies are always popular for birthday parties and any family or social gathering.

Preparation Time: 40 minutes

Portion Size: 24 servings

Ingredient List:

- 3 cups all-purpose flour, leveled
- 2 tsp. baking soda
- 1/2 tsp. salt
- 2/3 cup white sugar
- 1 cup brown sugar

- 1 cup chocolate chips, semi-sweet
- 1 cup dried cherries
- 1 tsp. vanilla extract
- 1 cup unsalted butter, and more for greasing
- 2 eggs

||||||||||||||||||||||||||||||||||||||||||||||||||||||||||||||||||

Methods:

Set oven to 350 degrees F and let preheat. Take a 9 by 5-inch baking pan, grease the bottom and inner sides with butter and set aside until required. Place butter and sugars in a bowl and using an electric beater, beat at high speed for 3 minutes or until fluffy. Then beat in eggs, one at a time, and vanilla until mixed. Then at low speed, gradually stir in flour until moist and thick batter comes together. Next, fold in chocolate chips and cherries and spoon the mixture into the prepared pan. Place pan into the oven and bake for 30 minutes or until inserted wooden skewer into the center of pan comes out clean. Let brownie cool on wire rack completely. Cut into squares and serve.

Recipe 26: Avocado Brownies

Avocado brownie is a perfect way to sneak in avocado into your meal. These brownies make a nutritious, heart-healthy and decadent dessert.

Preparation Time:35 minutes

Portion Size:16 servings

Ingredient List:

- 1 large avocado, peeled and cored
- 1/2 cup coconut flour
- 3 tbsp. ground flaxseed
- 1 tsp. baking soda
- 1/2 cup cocoa powder, unsweetened
- 1/4 tsp. salt
- 1/2 cup maple syrup

- 1 tsp. vanilla extract
- 3 eggs
- 1/2 cup applesauce, unsweetened
- 9 tbsp. water

||||||||||||||||||||||||||||||||||||||||||||||||||||||||||||||||||||||||||||||||

Methods:

Set oven to 350 degrees F and let preheat. In the meantime, take an 8-inch square baking pan, grease the bottom and sides with coconut oil and set aside until required. In a small bowl stir together flax seeds and water and let rest for 5 minutes. Cut avocado into bite size pieces and place in a blender. Add maple syrup, vanilla extract, and apple sauce and pulse until smooth. Transfer this mixture to a large bowl, add flax seeds mixture and whisk until combined. Stir in flour, salt, baking soda and cocoa powder until incorporated and thick dough comes together. Transfer dough to the prepared baking pan and place into the oven. Bake for 25 minutes or until done and inserted a wooden skewer into the center of the pan comes out clean. Let the brownie cool in the pan for 15 minutes before turning out to cool completely. Then cut into 16 squares and serve.

Recipe 27: Marshmallow Brownies

Soft and chewy marshmallow brownies are very simple to prepare and are a great dessert to serve family and friends.

Preparation Time:45 minutes

Portion Size:24 servings

Ingredient List:

- 5-ounce marshmallows, chopped
- 5-ounce plain flour
- 2-ounce caster sugar
- 2-ounce cocoa powder, unsweetened
- 5-ounce dark chocolate
- 8-ounce unsalted butter, and more for greasing the pan
- 5 eggs

Methods:

Set oven to 350 degrees F and let preheat. Take an 8-inch square baking pan, grease with butter. Line the greased pan with parchment sheet, leaving 2-inch of the sheet hanging from the sides, set aside until required. Place a medium-sized saucepan over medium-low heat, add butter and chocolate and let heat for 5 minutes or until chocolate melt completely, stirring frequently. In the meantime, in a bowl mix together flour, sugar, and cocoa until combined. Slowly whisk in the butter-chocolate mixture until incorporated and then mix in eggs until combined. Fold in marshmallows and spoon the mixture into the prepared pan. Place pan in the oven and bake for 20 to 25 minutes or until inserted wooden skewer into the center of pan comes out with moist crumbs. Let the brownie cool in pan for completely before turning it out. Cut into squares and serve.

Recipe 28: Chocolate Zucchini Brownies

These whole-grain chocolate brownies will be the gooiest brownies for those who never have tasted them. They are incredibly healthy and delicious that you won't feel these brownies have zucchini in them.

Preparation Time:45 minutes

Portion Size:16 servings

Ingredient List:

- ## 1 cup whole-wheat flour
  - 2 tbsp. ground flaxseed
  - 2 cups peeled and grated zucchini
  - 1/2 cup cocoa powder, unsweetened
  - 1 1/2 tsp. baking soda

- ## 3/4 cup coconut sugar
- 1 tbsp. vanilla extract
- 1/4 tsp. salt
- 6 tbsp. water
- 1/4 cup applesauce, unsweetened
- ## 1 cup vegan chocolate chips, semi-sweet
- 1/2 cup mini vegan chocolate chips

IIIIIIIIIIIIIIIIIIIIIIIIIIIIIIIIIIIIIIIIIIIIIIIIIIIIIIIIIIIIIIIIIIIII

Methods:

In a large bowl stir together flaxseed and water and let rest for 5 minutes. Set oven 350 degrees F temperature and let preheat. Take an 8-inch square baking pan, grease the bottom and sides with a non-stick cooking spray and set aside until required. In a medium-sized bowl place flour, add baking soda, salt, and cocoa powder and stir until well mixed. Into flax seed mixture, add sugar, vanilla and apple sauce, whisk until sugar dissolves completely. Then stir in flour mixture, 2 tbsp. at a time, until thick batter comes together, don't over mix. Then fold in 1 cup chocolate chips along with zucchini until combined and then transfer this mixture into the prepared pan. Smooth the top using a spatula and sprinkle mini chocolate chips over the top. Place pan into the oven and bake for 35 minutes or until done and inserted a wooden skewer into the center of pan comes out clean. Let brownie rest for 15 minutes and then turn out to cool completely. Then cut into 12 squares and serve.

Recipe 29: Sweet Potato Brownies

This brownie is a perfect way to present veggies as a decadent dessert. Sweet potato brownies are very tasty and nice.

Preparation Time: 45 minutes

Portion Size: 8 servings

Ingredient List:

- 1/2 sweet potato, cooked and pureed
- 1/2 carrot, cooked and pureed
- 1/2 cup almond flour
- 2 tbsp. cocoa powder, unsweetened
- 1/4 tsp. salt
- 1/4 cup powdered sugar
- 1/4 tsp. baking powder
- 2 cups chocolate chips, semi-sweet
- 1 tsp. vanilla extract
- 2 tbsp. olive oil

- 1 tbsp. silken tofu
- 1 tbsp. soy milk

||||||||||||||||||||||||||||||||||||||||||||||||||||||||||||||||||||||||

Methods:

Set oven to 350 degrees F and let preheat. Take an 8-inch square baking pan, grease the bottom and inner sides with a non-stick cooking spray and set aside until required. Place 1 1/2 cups chocolate chips in a microwave ovenproof bowl and microwave for 30 to 45 seconds or until melt completely, stir after 30 seconds. In a bowl, place flour and add salt, sugar, baking powder and cocoa powder. Stir until mixed well. In a separate big bowl tofu and milk and using a hand beater, beat until smooth. Then whisk in vanilla and oil until combined. Beat in flour mixture, 2 tbsp. at a time, or until incorporated. Fold in remaining chocolate chips and spoon the batter into the prepared pan. Place pan into the oven and bake for 25 to 30 minutes or until done and inserted a wooden skewer into the center of pan comes out clean. Let brownie cool for 15 minutes in the pan before turning out to cool completely. Cut into 8 squares and serve.

Chocolate-less Brownies

Recipe 30: Brown Sugar Brownies

Brown sugar brownie is an easy-to-prepare brownie with a slightly cakey texture. It is yummy and everyone will enjoy it.

Preparation Time: 35 minutes

Portion Size: 9 servings

Ingredient List:

- 1 cup all-purpose flour
- 1/4 tsp. salt
- 1 cup brown sugar
- 1/2 tsp. baking powder
- 1/2 cup nuts
- 1/2 cup unsalted butter, melted
- 1 tbsp. vanilla extract
- 1 tbsp. milk, unsweetened

- 1 egg

||||||||||||||||||||||||||||||||||||||||||||||||||||||||||||||||||||||||||||||||||||

Methods:

Set oven to 350 degrees F and let preheat. Take a 9-inch square baking pan, grease the bottom and sides with non-stick cooking spray and set aside until required. In the meantime, in a large bowl, place all the ingredients and whisk until combined. Spoon this mixture into the baking pan and use a spatula to smooth the top. Place baking pan into the oven and bake for 30 minutes or until done and inserted a skewer into the center of the pan comes out clean. Let the brownie cool in pan for 15 minutes before turning out to cool completely on a wire rack. Then cut into 9 wedges and serve.

Recipe 31: Applesauce Brownie

Incredibly tasty applesauce brownies only need four ingredients to come together without any baking. These brownies are flipping fantastic.

Preparation Time: 45 minutes

Portion Size: 12 servings

Ingredient List:

- ## 4-ounce coconut flour
  - 6 fluid ounce applesauce
  - 1/3 cup maple syrup
  - 2 tbsp. brown sugar

|||||||||||||||||||||||||||||||||||||||||||||||||||||||||||||||||||||||||

Methods:

Take a 6 by 6-inch baking pan, line with parchment sheet and set aside until required. In a bowl place all the ingredients and stir until incorporated and a thick dough comes together. Transfer the mixture into the prepared baking pan and smooth the top using the spatula. Sprinkle sugar over the top and place pan into the refrigerator for 30 minutes or until firm and set. Then, cut into 12 square of equal size and serve.

Recipe 32: Oatmeal Brownies

Chewy oatmeal brownies are a perfect fit as a healthy lunch box item for kids. Prepare in a large batch and have them any time of the day.

Preparation Time:45 minutes

Portion Size:16 servings

Ingredient List:

- 1 cup rolled oats, old-fashioned
- 1 1/2 cups baking mix, leveled
- 1/2 cup brown sugar
- 1/2 cup unsalted butter, and more for greasing pan
- 1 egg

||||||||||||||||||||||||||||||||||||||||||||||||||||||||||||||||||||||||||

Methods:

Set oven to 350 degrees F and let preheat. Take an 8-inch square baking pan, grease with butter, then line bottom with parchment sheet, grease it with butter and set aside until required. Place sugar in a medium bowl, add sugar and using an electric beater beat at medium speed until creamy. Then beat in egg until combined. Turn the speed of beater to low and gradually beat in baking mix until combined. Add 3/4 cup oats and stir until incorporated. Spoon this mixture into the prepared baking pan, smooth the top with a spatula and evenly sprinkle remaining oats over the top. Place pan into the oven and bake for 35 minutes or until done and a wooden skewer has come out clean when inserted it into the middle of the brownie. Let the brownie cool in the pan for 15 minutes before turning out to cool completely on wire rack. Then, cut into 16 squares and serve.

Recipe 33: Apple Brownies

Celebrate the fall season by preparing flavorful and delicious apple brownies. Any variety of apples will work for this recipe.

Preparation Time: 60 minutes

Portion Size: 12 servings

Ingredient List:

- 16-ounce apples, cored, peeled and cut into 1/2-inch pieces
- 1 cup all-purpose flour
- 1/2 tsp. salt
- 1 cup white sugar
- 1 tsp. ground cinnamon
- 1/4 tsp. baking soda
- 1/2 cup chopped walnuts

- 1/2 tsp. baking powder
- 4-ounce unsalted butter, melted
- 1 egg

||||||||||||||||||||||||||||||||||||||||||||||||||||||||||||||||||||||||||||||||||||||

Methods:

Set oven to 350 degrees F and let preheat until brownies are ready to bake. Take an 11-inch baking dish, grease the bottom and inner sides with non-stick cooking spray and set aside until required. In a medium bowl, place flour and add cinnamon, salt, baking powder and baking soda and stir until mix. In another bowl crack egg, add sugar and butter and using an electric beater, beat for 2 minutes or until frothy and combined. Add apple pieces and walnuts and stir using a spoon until combined. Stir in flour mixture, 2 tbsp. at a time, until incorporated. Spoon this mixture into prepared pan and smooth the top using a spatula. Place pan into the oven and bake for 40 minutes or until done and inserted a wooden skewer into brownie comes out clean. Let baked brownie cool in pan for 5 minutes before turning out to cool completely on a wire rack. Then, cut into 12 squares and serve.

Recipe 34: Pear and Pistachio Brownies

These healthy brownies feature the delicious taste of dried pears, crunchiness of pistachios and candied ginger. You can have it as a quick lunch or a tea-time snack.

Preparation Time: 60 minutes

Portion Size: 12 servings

Ingredient List:

- 3/4 cup chopped dried pears
- 1 2/3 cups all-purpose flour
- 1/4 cup chopped candied ginger
- 3/4 tsp. salt
- 1 cup brown sugar
- 1 tsp. baking powder
- 3/4 cup pistachios, chopped
- 1 tsp. vanilla extract
- 9 tbsp. unsalted butter, and more for greasing baking pan

- 2 eggs

||||||||||||||||||||||||||||||||||||||||||||||||||||||||||||||||||||||||||

Methods:

Set oven to 325 degrees F and let it preheat. Take a 9-inch round cake pan, and line the bottom and sides with a parchment sheet, leave 2-inch of the sheet hanging from the sides. Grease the parchment sheet with butter and set pan aside until required. In a medium bowl place flour, add salt and baking powder and stir until just mix, set aside until required. In a separate bowl place butter and sugar and using an electric beater beat at medium speed for 3 minutes or until creamy. Then beat in eggs and vanilla until combined. Then, switch speed of the beater to low and beat in prepared flour mixture, 2 tbsp. at a time, until incorporated. Fold in pears, ginger, and pistachios and spoon this mixture into prepared cake pan. Smooth the top with a spatula, and place pan into the oven. Bake for 50 minutes or until inserted wooden skewer into the center of pan comes out clean. Let it cool on the wire for 15 minutes before turning out to cool completely. Cut cake into wedges and serve.

Microwave Brownies

Recipe 35: Double Chocolate Brownies

The double chocolate brownie is a perfect last-minute dessert or snack for your chocolate or brownie cravings. Everyone will love these brownies.

Preparation Time: 12 minutes

Portion Size: 10 servings

Ingredient List:

- 1/2 cup all-purpose flour
- 1/4 tsp. salt
- 1 cup white sugar
- 2-ounce chocolate, unsweetened
- 1/2 cup semi-sweet chocolate chips
- 1/2 cup unsalted butter

- 1 tsp. vanilla extract
- 2 eggs, beaten

||||||||||||||||||||||||||||||||||||||||||||||||||||||||||||||||||||||||||

Methods:

Take an 8-inch microwave oven proof pan, place butter and chocolate and microwave for 2 minutes at high heat setting or until chocolate melt completely. Stir until smooth and then whisk in sugar until combined. Stir in flour, 1 tbsp. at a time, and salt and eggs until incorporated. Add vanilla until combined and fold in chocolate chips. Return pan to the microwave oven and microwave for 5 minutes at high heat setting or until done and inserted a wooden skewer into the brownie comes out clean. Let brownies stand 5 minutes before turning out from pan and then cut into ten squares using a sharp knife. Let brownies cool on a wire rack before serving.

Recipe 36: Triple Chocolate Mug Brownie

Try the fastest version to prepare the heavenly triple chocolate brownie using a microwave. It tastes exactly like the oven-baked version.

Preparation Time: 5 minutes

Portion Size: 1 serving

Ingredient List:

- 4 tbsp. all-purpose flour
- 1/8 tsp. salt
- 2 tbsp. white sugar
- 2 tbsp. cocoa powder, unsweetened
- ## 2 tbsp. chocolate chips
- 2 tbsp. melted butter, unsalted

- 1/4 tsp. vanilla extract
- 1 tbsp. chocolate syrup
- 2 tbsp. chocolate milk, unsweetened

||||||||||||||||||||||||||||||||||||||||||||||||||||||||||||||||||||||||

Methods:

In a microwave oven proof mug, place salt, vanilla, butter, and milk and stir until mixed well. Then stir in cocoa powder, 1 tbsp. at a time, and chocolate chips until mixed. Stir in sugar and then flour, 1 tbsp. at a time, until incorporated. Place mug in a microwave and microwave at high heat setting for 1 minute or until done and inserted a wooden skewer into the brownie comes out clean. Don't overcook the brownie. Let the brownie cool for 5 minutes, drizzle with chocolate syrup and serve.

Recipe 37: Mud Brownie

One word for this brownie, Yummy! Preparing mud brownie in a microwave oven is so easy and so good. Everyone in the family will love this decadent chocolate dessert.

Preparation Time: 20 minutes

Portion Size: 16 servings

Ingredient List:

- 3/4 cup all-purpose flour
- 1/4 cup and 3 tbsp. cocoa powder, unsweetened and divided
- 1 1/2 cups mini marshmallows
- 1/2 cup chopped pecans
- 1/8 tsp. salt
- 1 cup white sugar

- 2 cups of powdered sugar, sifted
- 1 1/2 tsp. vanilla extract, divided
- 3 tbsp. milk, unsweetened
- 3/4 cup butter, unsalted and divided
- 2 eggs, beaten

IIIIIIIIIIIIIIIIIIIIIIIIIIIIIIIIIIIIIIIIIIIIIIIIIIIIIIIIIIIIIIIIIIIIIIIIII

Methods:

Take a large microwave ovenproof bowl, add 1/2 cup butter and microwave on high heat setting for 1 minute or until butter melt completely. Whisk in white sugar and eggs until combined. Then stir in flour, 1 tbsp. at a time, and salt and 1/4 cup cocoa until incorporated. Stir in 1 tsp. vanilla and pecans. Take an 8-inch square baking dish, grease the bottom and sides with non-stick cooking spray. Spoon prepared brownie batter into the baking dish and then cover corners of the dish with aluminum foil. Place a microwave ovenproof bowl in a microwave oven, in inverted position, and then place baking dish on top of it. Microwave for 6 to 7 minutes at medium heat setting, turning dish after 3 minutes. Then, microwave at high heat setting for 2 to 3 minutes or until brownie is done and inserted wooden skewer into the brownie comes out clean. When the brownies are done, remove baking dish from the oven and sprinkle with marshmallows. Cover the dish with aluminum foil and let stand for 2 minutes. In the meantime, in a separate microwave ovenproof bowl place milk and remaining 1/4 cup butter and let heat at high heat setting for 2 minutes in a microwave or until butter melt completely. Whisk until smooth and then stir in remaining vanilla and cocoa powder until incorporated. Beat in powdered sugar with an electric beater, 2 tbsp. at a time until smooth. Spread this frosting mixture over the brownie, then cut into squares and serve.

Recipe 38: Chocolate Brownie

This ultimate dessert is crowd-pleasing. Moreover, it just takes 30 seconds to prepare. It is the fastest brownie you will ever make.

Preparation Time: 5 minutes

Portion Size: 1 serving

Ingredient List:

- 1 tbsp. all-purpose flour
- 1 tbsp. cocoa powder, unsweetened
- 1/8 tsp. salt
- 1 tbsp. brown sugar
- 1 tbsp. melted coconut oil
- 1 tbsp. water

Methods:

In a microwave oven proof mug, place all the ingredients and stir until mixed well. Then, place in a microwave and heat it at high temperature for 30 seconds or until done and inserted a wooden skewer into the brownie comes out clean. Don't overcook the brownie. Let brownie cool for 5 minutes before serving.

Recipe 39: Chocolate Glazed Brownie

This is a simple and quick recipe to prepare a fuss-free brownie. It tastes delicious!

Preparation Time:5 minutes

Portion Size:8 servings

Ingredient List:

- 1/2 cup all-purpose flour
- 2 tbsp. cocoa powder, unsweetened
- ## 3/4 cup semi-sweet chocolate chips
- 1/8 tsp. salt
- 1/2 cup white sugar
- 1/4 cup butter, unsalted
- 1 egg

- 1/2 tsp. vanilla extract

||||||||||||||||||||||||||||||||||||||||||||||||||||||||||||||||||||||||||||||

Methods:

Take a 4-inch square microwave ovenproof pan, grease the bottom and sides with a non-stick cooking spray and set aside until required. Place butter and cocoa in a microwave ovenproof bowl and microwave at high heat setting for 30 to 45 seconds or until melted. Stir until smooth and then whisk in flour, salt, sugar, egg, and vanilla until incorporated. Spoon the mixture into the prepared pan and smooth the top using a spatula. Place pan in a microwave and microwave at high heat setting for 2 to 3 minutes or until done and inserted a wooden skewer into the brownie comes out clean. When the brownies are done, remove the pan from the oven and sprinkle with chocolate chips immediately. Let brownies stand for 2 to 3 minutes and then cut into eight squares using a sharp knife before serving.

An Author's Afterthought

Did you like my book? I pondered it severely before releasing this book. Although the response has been overwhelming, it is always pleasing to see, read or hear a new comment. Thank you for reading this and I would love to hear your honest opinion about it. Furthermore, many people are searching for a unique book, and your feedback will help me gather the right books for my reading audience.

Thanks!

Printed in Great Britain
by Amazon

33021802R00059